A
King's Confession

New Look at Psalm 23

Lady Janice

ISBN: 978-1-09837-597-3 (printed)

ISBN: 978-1-09837-598-0 (eBook)

:

Table of Contents

CHAPTER ONE

Looking at Psalm 23 in New Way

Sticks and stones may break my bones; words will never hurt me. Whoever said that to us when I was a young girl, were flat-lying!

We are going to look at the 23rd Psalm in a new light. God has allowed me to see this in a fresh way. This is the Psalm read at funerals or when someone is deathly ill.

To comfort them.

If you are ready to learn something new from a man called after God's own heart. Prepare for your life to be transformed, then I will show you how this young man found some principles on the backside of the desert when he was out there tending his sheep doing his menial job.

I will show you something in the 23rd Psalm that David can teach us that he learned by understanding God's character when he was on the backside of the desert. He understood God's character more than a modern-day Christian; he had a deep understanding of God's character learned while doing his everyday menial task.

David discovered God's character and took on that nature. I am going to share these with you. We will break it into 3 sections; when life was good, everything great; then life got complicated, not so good; then his future life.

Like many psalms, Psalm 23 is used in both Jewish and Christian liturgies. It has been set to music often. It has been called the best-known of the psalms. For its universal theme of trust in God.

PSALM 23 IN ORIGINAL WRITING

מִזְמוֹר לְדָוִד: יְיָ רֹעִי, לֹא אֶחְסָר. בִּנְאוֹת דֶּשֶׁא יַרְבִּיצֵנִי,
עַל מֵי מְנֻחוֹת יְנַהֲלֵנִי. נַפְשִׁי יְשׁוֹבֵב. יַנְחֵנִי בְמַעְגְּלֵי צֶדֶק לְמַעַן
שְׁמוֹ. גַּם כִּי אֵלֵךְ בְּגֵיא צַלְמָוֶת לֹא אִירָא רָע, כִּי אַתָּה עִמָּדִי,
שִׁבְטְךָ וּמִשְׁעַנְתֶּךָ הֵמָּה יְנַחֲמֻנִי. תַּעֲרֹךְ לְפָנַי שֻׁלְחָן נֶגֶד צֹרְרָי,
דִּשַּׁנְתָּ בַשֶּׁמֶן רֹאשִׁי, כּוֹסִי רְוָיָה. אַךְ טוֹב וָחֶסֶד יִרְדְּפוּנִי כָּל
יְמֵי חַיָּי, וְשַׁבְתִּי בְּבֵית יְיָ לְאֹרֶךְ יָמִים.

PSALM 23

A Psalm by David.

1. The Lord is my Shepherd, I shall not want

2. He makes me lie down in green

pastures,

he leads me beside quiet waters,

3. he refreshes my soul.

He guides me along the right

paths

For his name's sake.

4. Even though I walk

through the darkest valley,

I will fear no evil,

for you are with me;

your rod and your staff,

They comfort me.

5. You prepare a table before me

In the presence of my enemies.

You anoint my head with oil;

My cup overflows.

6. Surely your goodness and

love will follow me

all the days of my life,

and I will dwell in the house of

the LORD

Forever.

- . The King of Love My Shepherd Is, THE LORD IS MY SHEPHERD

  - (Wikipedia)

How many reading this book know words are the most powerful things in the world. Scriptures tell us we are snared with the words of our mouth. The power of life and death is in the tongue. David understood some spiritual principles that words are potent containers, and you will have what you say and meditate repeatedly.

Our words are like the cocoon of a silkworm; you know, you can say some things, it really does not make that much difference, but you continue to say something over time, the length of our life and these words come up like a silk cocoon, and they bind us up.

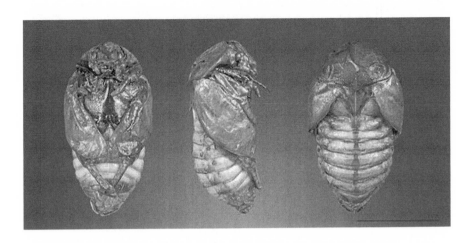

All the time, we are spinning a cocoon-like a silkworm,
You will have what you have been speaking, good or bad.

You say that is not fair. Fair or not, it is a spiritual principle that you violate it, and consequences are built into the violation. Same as gravity, you violate the law of gravity, and you will suffer consequences. There are spiritual laws God has in place; you violate them, and the consequences are built-in. You abuse your body; it will dilapidate on you. Speak negative, and you will have negative.

We speak a few things, and we can break out of that, and a few more weeks; after months, we find we cannot break out what we have been speaking. The scripture says you are snared by the words of your mouth, and it does not happen overnight; it occurs it occurs over time.

We are going to look at Psalm 23 in a different light. We will not look at it like a prayer that they say at funerals, but we will look at it as David's confession, his confession of life in life as a King.

All the time, we are spinning a cocoon-like a silkworm,

You will have what you have been speaking, good or bad.

The scripture says you are snared by the words of your mouth, and it does not happen overnight; it occurs throughout time.

PONDER THESE AND ANSWER TRUTHFULLY. CAN YOU RECALL YOUR WORDS YOU HAVE BEEN SPEAKING?

IS THERE ANYTHING YOU CAN CHANGE OF YOUR WORDS?

DO YOU NOT WANT YOUR LIFE TO WORK?

GOD CREATED YOUR LIFE TO WORK, BELIEVE IT, AND CHANGE. HOW WILL YOU DO THAT?

CHAPTER TWO

Epihpany Needs To Happen

David did not have Mark 11:23 "Truly I tell you, if anyone says to this mountain, 'Go, throw yourself into the sea,' and does not doubt in their heart but believes that what they say will happen, it will be done for them. NKJ

David did not have the New Testament but spent his early life on the backside of the desert singing psalms, hymns, and spiritual songs.

See the reason David could come down and fight Goliath when the men of Israel could not. It was because David learned how to deposit into his spirit words of encouragement and build himself up.

Lady Janice

Psalm 23 King James Version

The Lord is my Shepherd; I shall not want. 2 He makes me lie down in green pastures: he leadeth me beside the still waters. 3 He 8 Lady Janice restoreth my soul: he leadeth me in the paths of righteousness for his name's sake. 4 Yea, though I walk through the valley of the shadow of death, I will fear no evil: for thou art with me; thy rod and thy staff they comfort me. 5 Thou preparest a table before me in the presence of my enemies: thou anoint my head with oil; my cup runneth over. 6 Surely goodness and mercy shall follow me all the days of my life: and I will dwell in the house of the Lord forever.

Now, remember we are looking at this as David's confession in Psalm 23.

What David had been doing was prophesying his future. Did you know you can prophesy your future? All of us can.

As you speak things over some time, you are prophesying your future. You are establishing some things in your own spirit daily. We are painting images on the canvases of our hearts.

You ask, how do you do that? You take the tongue, which is the brush, you dip it in the word of God, which is the oil, and you paint an image of what your future is going to be on your heart.

You are all continually painting something onto your spirit. Proverbs 23:7.

7 For as he thinks in his heart, so is he.

So, we are continually spinning a cocoon, continuously painting pictures on the canvas of our hearts.

What you genuinely paint on your heart and meditate it, you will have it.

David was an expert artist; he learned to meditate on things and took Psalm 23 and sung it. Meditated it. Let us look at it in-depth and let the Spirit of the living God open up your mind to receive.

The theme of God as a shepherd was common in ancient Israel and Mesopotamia. For example, King Hamarubi, in conclusion to his famous legal code, wrote: "I am the shepherd who brings well-being and abundant prosperity; my rule is just.... so that the strong might not oppress the weak, and that even the orphan and the widow might be treated with justice."

This imagery and language were well known to the community that created the Psalm and was easily imported into its worship. (Wikipedia)

It was easy for David to know God. He knew God was his source. Here in Psalm 23, we are going to split it up into three sections.

PART ONE

The first part when everything is going really good. How many know it is easy to speak right and have a great confession when everything is going good? And you can say yes, the Lord is my Shepherd, praise God everything is going great. I got a full stomach, I have got a job, I have got health. It is easy to make a positive mouth confession when everything is going right. The Lord is my Shepherd. You need to understand David saw himself as a sheep because he was a shepherd.

Some of us know about shepherds, and some of us do not. In David's time, a shepherd caring for the sheep; loved every sheep, knew their personality, knew each one's characteristic.

It is known that the Shepherd knows each sheep by name; thus, when God is given the analogy of a shepherd, he is not only a protector but also the caretaker. God, as the caretaker, leads the sheep to green pastures (verse 2) and still waters (verse 2) because he knows that each of his sheep must be personally led to be fed.

Thus, without its Shepherd, the sheep would die either by a predator or of starvation. Since sheep are known for their helplessness without their Shepherd.

The Shepherd loved them so very much he knew their names the same way God knows us, loves us, and knows our name.

How many know the redemptive names of Jehovah. One characteristic of God is Jehovah Rohi; the Lord is my Shepherd.

Jesus said I am the Good Shepherd. A Good Shepherd lays down his life for his sheep, so David had a good understanding of God's characteristics. he says, I am a sheep, God is my Shepherd, and he is a Good Shepherd. The Lord is my Shepherd.

I could ask you, reading this book, is he your Shepherd? Now I am not asking you if he is your Lord. I am asking you is he your Shepherd. See, David understood some things about God's character. Some Christians think God is always out to get them. You know you step out of line, and God's going to do this; put sickness on, you take your kids away from you, take your money. If you believe God is that type of God, you cannot say the Lord is your Shepherd because God's a Good Shepherd, and a Good Shepherd cares for his sheep intimately.

The Shepherd desires to see his sheep prosper, not put sickness on them. Not put them down some ravine somewhere, but the Lord is my Shepherd. Keeping in mind, David is painting a picture onto the canvass of his heart. The Lord is the Shepherd I shall not want.

That is a very bold confession. If you can say that I shall not lack, that is a bold confession. If you honestly say that and mean it. Make that with the mouth, and believe it with your heart. Say it now to yourself out loud to I shall not lack for the rest of my life. Maybe half of the people reading this book could; the rest give mental assent to that confession.

I mean, say it, and really mean it from your heart. Saying it, I shall not lack, not like empty words.

David is on the backside of the desert; no one can hear him. How many know out of the abundance of the heart the mouth speaks. He speaks out of the abundance of his heart: The Lord is my Shepherd, and he's probably singing it. I shall not lack, I shall not lack, I shall not lack for the rest of my life.

Let me give you a little secret David never lacked.

It is interesting to note that David never lacked; even when he was running from Saul. he never lacked. He was always provided for. The Lord is the Shepherd I shall not lack; I shall not lack. David saw him as that sheep.

That word, the Lord is my Shepherd, literally means the Lord shall provide Jehovah Jireh...

The Lord will provide. God always speaks to us in ways we understand; that's how God spoke to David. Let me share something about shepherds in the day in time that David lived. In that period, the shepherds in those days, as they walked along, would break the twigs with the leaves off the trees and pick up little pieces of grass. They would feed the sheep that were the closest to them, and so it was a sheep that was always closest to the Shepherd who got the best fed.

The ones who kept in close the Shepherd would make sure they were provided with all the little goodies, the same way with us; those who stay the closest to the Lord are the best fed. When you drift away, you will get skinny on us, and no, this is not a new diet fad where O well, I know how to get slim.

Now, listen to me; the sheep understood the voice of the Shepherd. And when the Shepherd would come into a town and gather for rest and fellowship, play cards or just talk, wherever at night. All the sheep would be put in one big pen and mingle together, and they would all get mixed up.

Now Can you imagine 100 shepherds and 10,000 sheep? When it was time to go the following day, how would you go out there and find which ones are your sheep?

All the Shepherd had to do was go out there and speak; his sheep would respond to his voice and voice alone. No other Shepherd could get the sheep to respond. Only his sheep would respond to his voice.

The Bible **John 10:27** My sheep know my voice, and I know them. They follow me. How many reading this book have heard the voice of God? How many recognize his voice? I mean, you know when God is speaking to you and when you respond, things will happen.

David said, the Lord is my Shepherd I shall not lack; he makes me lie down in green pastures. To me, green pastures speak of provision and plenty.

And I believe David was speaking out of what he had been producing on the image of his heart: The Lord is the Shepherd I shall not want. He makes me lie down in green pastures. I can see my home green pastures, see my family, my church, my business, everything I am involved in is to be green pastures.

Victorious, you need to understand and say my God shall supply all my needs. I want you to repeat it, we are artists continually painting a picture of our future life onto the canvas of our hearts.

David is a master at this; not only does he have the ability to paint a beautiful picture of his own spirit, but he can do it to his followers, his men.

Remember, he had 300 men come to him at Cave Addulum.

You can find that first Samuel 30. we have looked at David we found where David lived in cave Addulum. Everyone that was in distress, debt, and discontented, everyone gathered themselves unto David. David became a captain over them; we see through some procedures how David transformed those in distress debt and discontented into his mighty men.

Something happened there. David's life so far had been one of obscurity as a Shepherd boy, and then he was thrust into fame. You will find where he starts off as a Shepherd boy in the desert, then he gets into the fight of his life with Goliath, and from that point on, David is thrust into fame in Jerusalem. And you too can learn how to change your life by looking at the example of King David; when he was a Shepherd boy, he learned these, and I want to share that with you. More in-depth in a new book, THE CONTENDERS.

Right now, we see the beginnings of a King, a great KING of Israel. King David. Started on the backside of the desert by himself and his sheep. No one there to impress. God said despise not thy small beginnings. The Lord is my Shepherd. I shall not want He makes me lie down in green pastures; he leads me beside the still water. The waters of quietness literally, that is what it means. Tranquil waters ..psychiatrist will tell you that if you are stressed, you've got problems, and you have things that bother and make you anxious. You are just so worried it is hard to live. They will tell you to get you a giant aquarium and get you some tropical fish and watch them. They have a calming effect on your soul.

When I am troubled, I like to go by Lake, sit down, meditate, and watch the water, especially when it is smooth like glass. He leads me beside the still and restful waters, waters of quietness, waters of tranquility. Again, I believe that he's prophesying about his future; he's not only speaking about provision but about peace. What is one of the fruit of the spirit?

Peace David didn't have the book of Galatians to learn about the fruit of the spirit. Still, he knew and understood some things he learned from his Father about peace and tranquility. And he is showing us the way we can produce peace in our own hearts. We need to be like David and speak in terms of peace, provision, joy, Faith, and protection.

Just listen, sometimes to some Christians talk. It will amaze you how they talk about how their life will be; they say, well blessed God, I am always in trouble, I'm always in a crisis. Gods putting me through valleys always.

Nothing works for me; I am always going through the smoke, the fire, in the mud. Well, what sort of image are YOU continually painting on YOUR spirit? It does not surprise me that so many Christians are going through a continual crisis in their lives.

Because that is the way they continually speak over and over and over. They are repeatedly painting pictures literally upon their hearts.

Do you understand what you have just read?

NOTE:

_____

_____

CHAPTER THREE

Learn How To Have Ordered Speech

The Bible says, let the weak say I am strong; why do you think God tells us to talk in those terms? Let the weak say I am strong! My God shall supply all my needs according to his riches and glory, that I will not lack? Because you will be continually producing it. You are a producer. You were made to be a producer; we need to give a wonderful affirmation of God's love and God's care and God's concern like David did.

He makes me lie down in green pastures, leads me beside the still waters; just close your eyes for a minute and think about what you have read so far. And I want to show you how you could meditate the word of God; he makes me lie down in green pastures. Now see that with your eyes shut. See, he makes me lie down in green pastures. Can you see the sheep out there, content continually feeding in green pastures? My homes are green pasture.

My families a green pasture. My church, my ministry my, health my, business.

Everything that concerns me is a green pasture he leads me beside the still and restful waters.

When you are plagued, and you're tired, and you need rest, you need to come back to the word of God. Go to Psalm 23 and meditate and speak it out. Just thinking about it is not going to do any good. You have got to speak it out. How many know green pastures do not just happen. It takes great effort to produce green pastures; the ground must be plowed up, rocks have to be gotten rid of them, have to be watered, irrigated. There is much to be done to prepare for green pastures, same as with you.

You must put the time in for you to grow and be successful. Some Christians think they can say whatever they like to think, and they will have green pastures. No, no, no, you will have to have preparation time, spend time in the word of God, meditating the word of God speaking the word of God. You will have to develop some things in your spirit before saying my entire family is a green pasture.

How many know we need to speak blessing instead of cursing? I did not say cussing; I said cursing. You are either part of the answer, or you're part of the problem. It is what you speak out of your mouth; every word the Bible says, by your words, you will be justified or condemn not just one day.

But we are all like a silkworm producing and spinning every day, but our words will either protect us or bind us up. I talk with people, saying, hey, I find things are just not going right suddenly. Well, listen to their words the last two or three years, and you will find out exactly why things are not going right. You are the sum total of what you've been saying you are. Did you hear me?

You are the sum total of what you've been saying you are; you live in the result of your speaking for the last few years, right now. You say that is not fair. I do not care whether it's fair; it's a fact. You are living in the sum total of what you have released from your mouth over the past few years; I love David; he understood this. Look at all the problems David had.

He could have said, well, you know whether or not the Lord is my Shepherd, I've got to go fight Goliath I got to get rid of Saul I got to go there do, this just crisis crisis crisis, not David.

David said, the Lord is my Shepherd I shall not lack; he leads me beside the still and restful waters. I love the way David can paint a picture; that is why I love to go back over it myself every so often.

He said he restores my soul; I believe in restorative theology. How many have ever been so tired, beaten down, and depressed, and when you are tired, you are so depressed, the last thing you want to do come to God. That is the last thing you want to do is to pray.

Be honest with yourself; you do not want to pray; you don't want to study the word of God. David said he restores my soul. God's a Good Shepherd that he cares for us; you know if you let the word speak to you; it speaks words of encouragement, words of life and love. Remember the story of the prodigal son he came back.

The Father came out and made him welcome, encouraged and lifted him up.

What about Peter when he denied the Lord three times. Did Jesus condemn him? No, he took him back and loved him just as if nothing ever happened.

Psalm 34:2says, see, God will lift you up if you let God's word get into your spirit, meditating and speak it and start to live it.

You praise God; that is why it talks about the sacrifice of praise every day. Start your day with the sacrifice of praise; you will find it will start to change the way you think. PSALM 86:4 Rejoice the soul of thy servant: for unto thee, O Lord, do I lift up my soul.

We get that word in us, and it begins to lift us up, refresh us, and restores our emotional realm.

THINK ON GODS WORD, SAY OVER AND OVER. LET THE WORDS LIFT AND REFRESH YOU.

DID YOU DO THAT?_____

_____

CHAPTER FOUR

Learn How To Live Really Live

We are three-part beings; we have a spirit, a soul, and the body. And the soul is your emotional realm where your imaginations, emotions, and intellect are. Where you make decisions. It works for me when I am down. I like to go to my room and meditate on the word of God. I take scriptures that speak vividly to me.

I want to speak them out because they paint a picture, and I hear them. Who are you going to believe in your voice or somebody else? The Lord is my Shepherd; I like to speak it until it paints a picture; I shall not lack a wonderful church family's provisions for health I paint with my mouth. I shall not lack for health even if I am sick. I'm going to paint that picture and then look at it.

Psalm 2:3 and a saying it over and over really, that is meditating the word.

I paint the picture I repeatedly want and Meditating it, murmuring speaking the word.

Most Christians paint pictures of wrong, anxiety about what will happen if the money doesn't come in lack, poverty, or death. What's going to happen? Worry, doubt, fear is what your painting pictures repeatedly on your spirit when you speak. Whether now or in the past, every one of us either had success in painting pictures we do not want to be called, fear and worry.

Continuing, 23: 3b he leads me in the path of righteousness,

How many know the Holy Spirit leads? I hear people say the Holy Spirit made me do this or do that. I cannot find one place where the Holy Spirit made anybody do anything. Did you hear what I said? Now demon

spirits, they will push and shove. But the Bible says the Holy Spirit leads. The Holy Spirit will never make you do anything. Did he make you get saved? Did he make you get up and go to church to worship?

People will come and say, I want to be filled with the Holy Ghost. They say I'm going to stay in right here until the Holy Ghost makes me speak in tongues; well, most people are just still standing there unless they got too tired went home. Because the Holy Spirit will never make you do anything, he will lead you and guide you.

Anytime you're being pushed and shoved, it is not the Holy Spirit. Anything that takes your peace away is not the Holy Spirit; it is demonic. Holy Spirit leads you; the Holy Spirit will guide you and direct you, but you have to be a follower.

If you're going to be LED, you've got a choice you choose. I set before you this day the choice of life and death; let's say the Holy Spirit led you to buy this book, but you didn't have to. It was your choice to buy this book he leaves that to you. It so essential that we learn to follow. Some folks say I'm lead of the Lord, and, sometimes, that is the biggest joke you've ever heard in your life. They're not letting the Lord lead them. Most Christians are not led by the Lord; they let their feelings and emotions lead, and they want God to rubber-stamp whatever they want to do.

You find many people are unteachable; they are stiff neck; they wallow in their old habits. They give mental assent to the word, and mental assent; means we agree with God's word; we just don't want to do it.

You must bring your feelings, your life, your actions all to line up with the word of God. You must do that because God's word is truth, and we are never to base what we believe on what we see or what we think, except what the word says. If you can bring your Faith to line up with what the word says, you'll find that your life works, and you will start to walk in the spirit. You will be spirit lead regardless of the circumstances or how you feel; if the Bible says you are strong, then you are strong.

If the word says he will never leave you nor forsake you, then he will never leave you nor forsake you. And I sometimes know many people feel like God left them, I have, but he never left. He's always been right there, never. Never has he left me in all my born-again life. Did you hear what I said? Born again. Like he said, he wouldn't, and he didn't. David understood that he leads me in paths of righteousness. But that's your choice to follow. The Holy Spirit will always lead us and lead us to God. The Holy Spirit will always lead you in victory; the Holy Spirit will always lead me in triumph.

Did you know losing is foreign nature to God? Can you find in scriptures one time God lost, so why is it we accept it? Being losers totally against God's nature to fail. And when we're born again, we get our nature from my Papa, our parent's right. Is it normal for a dog to bark? It's abnormal if you have a baby dog and they don't bark. If you have a fish and it doesn't want to swim, that's very abnormal that your fish will not swim. Does God always win?

Then it is unnatural for a Christian to lose. Completely out of character for a born-again Christian to fail at anything. Now that goes cross-grained to religion and our feelings and teaching that's been taught. It is true.

If we follow what the Bible says, thanks be to God, who always leads me in triumph. Do you believe the word? Well, it says he always leads us in triumph in every area, church, home, relationships, business, all areas of walking in triumph. Right? Every one of us can learn how to walk and be led by the Holy Spirit. The more you will walk in victory.

According to Strong's Concordance, the Greek word most often translated as "overcomer" stems from the word Nike, which means "to carry off the victory." The verb implies a battle." The Bible teaches Christians

to recognize that the world is a battleground, not a playground. God does not leave us defenseless.

Have you read the word today?

HAVE YOU PUT ON THE ARMOR OF GOD? ARE YOU DETERMINED TO SUCCEED IN EVERYTHING THROUGH JESUS CHRIST?

_____

_____

Note what changes you will make.:

_____

_____

CHAPTER FIVE

Things Have Changed, Now What?

We've been looking at where things had been going fine, and his confession was great. That's easy to have praise God bless God's confession when all is going good. Now when things change, your confession should not. David speaks of times of trouble. One thing you will find about David when circumstances changed, his mouth confession does not.

Psalm 23: 3-b-4-b He restores my soul; He leads me in the paths of righteousness For His namesake,

4. though I walk through the valley of the shadow of death, I will fear no evil; For You *are* with me; Your rod and your staff, they comfort me. He leads me in the paths of righteousness, for His name's sake.

SECOND PART: When you see circumstances change, your Faith's confession in God's word must not. Now David speaks of trouble; this is the second part one of Psalm 23, the thing you'll find about David; he understood God did not change, so he did not change his confession.

And circumstances will change, but the mouth confession doesn't have to. David's confession did not change, even though he saw the trouble. I know most Christians, when their situation changes, so does their mouth.

Here in verse 4, David understood God. Even though I walk through the valley of the shadow of death, how many know **it's not** the valley of death. Christians will never taste death. It's the shadow, and Satan's will try to bring fear in your life at some stage. But God said he did not give us a spirit of fear but of power, love, and a sound mind.

Just know, at some stage, everyone reading this book will go through the valley of the shadow of death. Some people think the message of Faith releases them from problems or troubles. We will have tribulations and situations in this life, but through Jesus Christ, we will overcome them, or we can if we choose God's Word.

Yes, we were told we would be successful and overcome, but you will have to choose what you will do when going through tribulation. But we will overcome. David said I will fear no evil. How many know without Faith, it is impossible to please God.? How many know that it's easy to confess praise God when everything is going well. The Bible tells us and teaches us to hold fast to our profession of Faith.

Never let it go but hold fast to your confession of Faith. There are 365 scriptures in the word of God speaking against fear. Why? Because fear is the most destructive force on this planet.

Fear is the most destructive force on this planet, so Satan uses fear more than any other opposing force in the Bible. You find so often when Christ came to minister, he would say fear not. Fear and Faith are opposing forces. One pleases God, and the other will destroy you.

Fear not. He doesn't say hate, not bitter not, he said fear not. Because fear will destroy your Faith quicker than anything. You cannot have Faith and fear together; they are opposing forces. Have one or the other. That's what Jesus constantly spoke, fear not, fear not. Do not let fear come upon you. As I walk through the valley of the shadow of death, David said I'll just lie down or just die right now, wallow in self-pity. No, he never said that. He never said, oh, I'll never make it.

No, David said, though I walk through, walkthrough, I will go through. David understood some things. He said I might go through some things, but I will go through them.I won't stay there, I won't lie down, I will not wallow in it. Yea, though, I walk through the valley of the shadow of death. See, David had a picture of him going through the problem.

See yourself going through a problem, through- beyond, it no matter what the situation.See yourself passing through the problem, not staying in it. David knew GOD would give him safe passage. David had a better understanding of God's character and nature than most modern-day Christians do.

Safe passage, know why he had safe passage? Because the Lord is my Shepherd I shall not lack if I go through the valley of the shadow of death, I will pass through it, for he will never leave me nor forsake me, I fear evil.

Verse-4B- who knows what the rod represents? The word of God.

See, the rod was an extension of Shepherd's authority. When he walked along, that rod extended his authority. His hand could not reach over to punch all the Wolves and other predators, but his rod could. He could take that rod and, bong, bong hit them on the head to protect his sheep.

The rod was an extension of his authority; the rod represents the word, and the word is given to us to use. It is not given to us to destroy one another. When Jesus was tempted by the biggest enemy, he said it is written!

We're not to use it against each other, but against the enemy. The Shepherd had two things: a rod and the staff. The rod was used to defend the sheep. The staff was used to look after the sheep.

The rod is symbolic of the word of God; the staff is symbolic of the Holy Spirit.

I found this very interesting he never used the staff to beat the sheep; the staff was used to touch and encourage the sheep while looking after the sheep. The staff always used to touch the sheep to encourage the sheep while the Shepherd was looking after them. Never used as a weapon, never used on the sheep. It was used to defend the sheep.

How many know you need to pray the word of God, use the word of God.

What did Jesus use when Satan came against him, he used the word of God? You pray the word of God to speak the word of God. and we need to meditate the word of God. Now the staff represents the Holy Spirit. What a combination of the Holy Spirit and the word of God, which the rod represents.

The rod was the offensive weapon, the staff, the Holy Spirit, was used to guide, direct and lead the sheep.

Some Christians believe our wonderful Gods will discipline them with sickness car wrecks, lose everything, believe that. God just waiting to crush them like a ghetto cockroach to correct me.

If you believe that, you have a perverted view of our loving God.

GOD USES HIS WORD to chastise, correct and discipline his children, the believers.

GOD doesn't have condemnation; he uses conviction of the drawing power of the Holy Spirit. That is how he will speak to you if you listen.

For example, you get out of line and miss the mark of what God wants for you. Do you need someone to come and tell you what you did wrong? We all have gotten out of line, and we knew we missed it with God. did you need to be told you missed it or did the Holy Spirit come to gently and give you a scripture to show you where you were out of line.

See, David understood what we need to understand.

Jesus came into the world to seek and save that which was lost. Jesus uses convicting power, never CONDEMNATION.

Condemnation comes from Satan. His job is to kill, steal and destroy you. Anytime that happens, it is from the enemy. Use the Word of God to fight your battles. First, you must learn and believe what God says is true. David did. Look how his life was transformed.

ARE YOU A BELIEVER?

WHAT IS COMING AGAINST YOU, TO MAKE YOU CHANGE YOUR WORDS INTO NEGATIVE ONES

CHAPTER SIX

In Your Face Enemies

PSALM VERSE 5 Thou preparest a table before me in the presence of mine enemies: thou anoints my head with oil; my cup runneth over.

David is planning his future life now; thou prepare a table before me in the presence of my enemies.

Let me say this: many Christians are demon happy. Demon crazy-everything's a demon. Some people that's all they talk about is demons, demons, demons, demons; there are only three things you really need to know about Satan,

1. He is nothing

2. Has nothing

3. He can do nothing.

Listen, when you walk with God in the anointing's power of God, there is nothing, absolutely nothing Satan and his demons can do about it. If they could, they would have prevented you from being saved,

He has no power unless you give it to him. The power he has, we have usually given him to him. He is nothing but unemployed cherubim. He cannot have any power or authority over you and can't do anything unless you surrender it to him. And David understood that.

David understood this! Unless you surrender your authority, Satan can do nothing.

David said he prepares a table in my enemies' presence, not my friends, my enemies.

Lady Janice

Verses 4 and 5 King David acknowledges God's protection in expeditions and in battles.

"Thou preparest a table before me in the presence of mine enemies" refers to the sober raucous dinner before significant battles. These were raucous in order to demoralize hostiles camped within earshot, and (only) the king ate from a table. "Thou anointest my head with oil" because tomorrow this ceremony might be impossible.

After each victory, so "my cup runneth over." The king's lyricist wisely shortened these military verses for balance. Also, in Psalm 18, David mentions God's protection in battle.

The first verse of the Psalm ascribes authorship to King David. Said in the Hebrew Scriptures, David had been a field shepherd himself as a youth.

Taken together, Psalm 22, 23 and 24, is seen by some as shepherd psalms,

The good Shepherd lays down his life for the sheep as a suffering servant to become a King.

Listen, when you walk with God in the anointing's power of God, there is nothing, absolutely nothing Satan and his demons can do about it. If they could, they would have prevented you from being saved. And David understood that. A table is prepared. In my enemies' presence, he said my enemies didn't say my friends; he said, my enemies.

When you walk with God in power and the anointing of God, Satan and his demons can do nothing about it; if there was, they would have stopped you from getting saved.

Right? he prepares a table; in other words, your needs are met; every need is met right in the very presence of your enemies. Does not matter if demons all around you, or you are in downtown Bali and you are by the monkey temple. It does not make a bit of difference because God prepares a table before you in the presence of your enemies!

The monkey temple is all around you doesn't matter. Now prepare a table before me in the presence of my enemies. You get a revelation, an accurate understanding; when you walk in God's word, know the word of God, there is nothing Satan and his cohorts can do.

Thou Hast anointed my head with oil. In biblical times, they always anointed the winner in Olympic games with oil. How many reading this knows God sees us as a winner. You know why because it is his nature to win, and we are his children. If believers did what God instructs us to, you would win. They anointed the winner's head with oil.

How many know that God sees you as a winner through JESUS CHRIST. And it is in his nature to win, and we as his offspring are to be winners. If you do what God says, you will succeed in everything you set your hand to, and you can be successful.

God said to Joshua, if you want to succeed in every area of your life, meditate on my word and be obedient to it. You can be successful in whatever you put your hand to.

I believe that's how God sees us, and that's how David saw himself. My head is anointed with oil, and my cup runs over now.

CHAPTER SEVEN

We Are More Than Conquerors

Now, the third phase of David's confession:

Psalm 23:6 Only goodness and mercy pursue me, All the days of my life, and my dwelling [is] in the house of Jehovah, For a length of days!

Let's look at the third phase of David's confession. In **the first phase, things were going good**. In the **second phase, things not going so good**, and now the **third phase is for the future.**

The **word surely** is one of the most positive and most potent words in the English language. Surely means a guarantee without a doubt. It's a sure thing positive. Surely goodness and mercy will follow me.

See David; he's understood God's character. He didn't say problems, sickness crisis, looking for a job, never having my needs met, but he surely said goodness and mercy will follow me. Now David was on the backside of the desert when he was making this confession. This is going to be his future life, surely goodness and mercy. If you follow David's life, you will see he missed it many times with God. he had doubts and difficulties. Goodness and mercy followed him. Even though David missed it many times, you will notice something else as you study David's life. It does not mean only goodness and mercy will follow David and to David, but goodness and mercy will flow from David. Remember Jonathan's son when Saul's family was completely wiped out?

David said, is there anyone from the family left alive, any at all. They found Jonathan's son and brought him back to David because of David and Jonathan's covenant. And he told this young man.

According to the biblical narrative (2 Samuel 4:4), Mephibosheth was five years old when both his Father and grandfather died at Gilboa... After the deaths of Saul and Jonathan, Mephibosheth's nurse took him and fled in panic. In her haste, the child fell or was dropped while fleeing. After that, he was unable to walk

Some years later, after his accession to the kingship of King David, he sought someone of Saul's house, to whom I may show the kindness of God," and Mephibosheth was brought to him. David restored Saul's inheritance to Mephibosheth and permitted him to live within his palace in Jerusalem.

David said You will dwell in my house for the rest of your life, even though this son saw himself as an enemy to David. David had goodness and mercy flowing from his life, and he had goodness and mercy flowing into his life. It not only followed him, but it flowed from him; surely only goodness and mercy will follow me all the days of my life.

What a confession David had. Can you have that confession that goodness and mercy will follow you all the days of your life and flow out

from your life? You, me yes, we've all got problems. I've had problems, but what's the rest of your life going to be like. Surely goodness and mercy will follow me all the days of my life. Do you know what David was doing?

He's giving a wonderful affirmation of God's incredible ability to produce victory and success in his life, surely only goodness and mercy? David is painting a picture on his heart. David did not sing or say this once and forget it I honestly believe David kept saying this perhaps a dozen times a day every day of his life.

You know you can only speak things that are abundant in your heart. David's out there on the backside of the desert. No one to hear him. He's not going to just start off with a positive mouth confession to impress everybody in life like most do. No one is out there .he is saying what he is really thinking in his heart. How many know when you're out by yourself, you will say what you really mean.

David really believes ,only surely, and goodness would follow him all the days of his life because he painted a picture; he painted a picture onto his spirit onto his heart.

He's talking about his future PSALM 23:6. Surely goodness and mercy shall follow me all the days of my life, and I will dwell in the House of the Lord forever. Some reading this book could probably say this for maybe three weeks.

But David is talking about his life after death. Let me ask you, now really think about this no positive confession, just ask yourself, if I were to die, where would I go? Would I go be with the Lord? If you can't say that, you need to reconcile that today.

THERE IS A DIFFERENCE OF CHARACTER AND REPUTATION. REPUTATION IS WHAT OTHERS THINK OF YOU.

CHARACTER IS WHAT YOU ARE REGARDLESS OF WHO IS AROUND.

WHICH DO YOU HAVE? CHARACTER? _____

REPUTATION? _____

CHAPTER EIGHT

You Can Really Have a Kingly Life

Y ou need to know that, like David did without the slightest doubt, you would go straight to be with the Father, for that's where you belong, for you came from him. And you will return to him.

David's not even born again, no one was born again until Jesus came, but David had such a trust in his Father God, he said the Lord is my Shepherd. I know he's a Good Shepherd and will give his life for me. The only watch is over to protect me and provide me with success in my life; he said not only now but forever this man, who was not born again, could say that.

But yet there are many born-again Christians who cannot even say that. They do not have the confidence. They think somewhere down the road, I might miss it and not make it to heaven. Many reading this book can't say that people will say what they really believe in private times. I've had people come to me and say I don't know if I'm really saved. I don't know if I would even go to heaven.

Well, you can learn from David; you're like a silkworm spinning and prophesying your future. You're speaking out of the abundance of your heart. What will you be able to say, surely goodness and mercy, or perhaps you say sickness, unemployment can you say peace, or is it frustration, joy or bitterness and hate?

You can have an abundant life now and for all eternity. Ask Jesus to be your Lord and Savior today. And confess a good confession every day of your life. The Lord is my Shepherd.

I really want you to learn to say; my life is a green pasture. You say, but I'm not sure about that; it's on rocky grounds right now I might not make it.

Well, you need to paint and give a wonderful affirmation daily of God's power to change your life for his glory to be what you expect your future to be that only goodness and mercy follow you that you will dwell in the House of the Lord forever I want you to read Psalm 23 and confess it daily not let it be just the empty thing off the top of your head.

Please do not just give mental assent but continually doing it to paint a picture in your heart, until an image you see and can say; out of the abundance of your heart your mouth will speak; you should attempt to paint on the canvas of your heart words of goodness and mercy.

NOW CALL TO ACTION:

Now you need to read Psalm 23 two times a day at least for 40 days and then make it a lifestyle; when you do this, you will spin a cocoon with words that you speak that won't bind you but will make you successful all the days of your life

---

does not matter if demons are all around you doesn't matter what's going on that surely goodness and mercy will follow you all the days of your life because the Lord is your

Shepherd. I pray the Lord to bless you and his face shine upon you until we meet again in heaven. I ask God to bless you for reading this book.

There is a sequel coming out about David's Mighty Men. When they came to David, they were men in debt, angry, bitter, murderers, and on. Their lives were changed when they went to the place David could show them how to change.

Hope to see you in the book CONTENDERS.

Thank you for reading this book, and I trust you will adhere to what King David did and begin to see life so that people will ask you what HAS HAPPENED.

Get in the Bible and learn of King Jesus, the most excellent Shepherd of all times. Allow him to be your Lord and Shepherd.

In the Gospel of John, Jesus states, "I am the good shepherd" in two verses, John 10:11 and 10:14

I am the good Shepherd. The good Shepherd lays down his life for the sheep. A hired hand and not a shepherd, who doesn't own the sheep, sees the wolf coming, leaves the sheep, and flees.

The wolf snatches the sheep and scatters them. The hired hand flees because he is a hired hand and doesn't care for the sheep. I am the good Shepherd. I know my own, and I'm known by my own; even as the Father knows me, and I know the Father.

I lay down my life for the sheep. I have other sheep, which are not of this fold. I must bring them also, and they will hear my voice. They will become one flock with one Shepherd.

Therefore, the Father loves me because I lay down my life, that I may retake it. No one takes it away from me, but I lay it down by myself. I have the power to lay it down, and I have the power to take it again. I received this commandment from my Father. John 10: 11-18.

Today make him your Lord and Savior, repeat this prayer, and mean it.

My desire is for you to take action and ensure your eternal life and life abundantly now.

Lord Jesus, I thankyou so much for loving me enough to die on the cross. Your precious blood washes me clean of every sin. Every sin I have ever done is gone and forgiven. I accept you as my Lord and My Savior now and forever. I believe that you rose from the dead and that you are ALIVE TODAY. Because of your finished work, I am now a beloved child of God, and heaven is my home. Thank you for giving me eternal life and filling my heart with peace and joy. And leading me all the days of my life for your will and purpose. I give myself to you by my choice. Amen.

Lady Janice

Contact me for further information.

Lady Janice @hallelujahlady.com

ALL FOR THE GLORY OF GOD.HIS GLORY SHALL FILL THE EARTH!